# After Swissair

# Budge Wilson

Pottersfield Press, Lawrencetown Beach, Nova Scotia, Canada

Library and Archives Canada Cataloguing in Publication

Wilson, Budge, author
    After Swissair / Budge Wilson.
Poems.
ISBN 978-1-897426-81-4 (paperback)
    1. Swissair Flight 111 Crash, 1998--Poetry.  I. Title.
PS8595.I5813A38 2016      C811'.54      C2015-907585-8

Cover photo: Sea Change, an original quilt designed and made by Barb Robson

Pottersfield Press acknowledges the financial support of the Government of Canada through the Canada Book Fund for our publishing activities. We acknowledge the support of the Canada Council for the Arts. Nous remercions le Conseil des arts du Canada de son soutien. We are pleased to work in partnership with the Province of Nova Scotia to develop and promote our creative industries for the benefit of all Nova Scotians.

Pottersfield Press
83 Leslie Road
East Lawrencetown, Nova Scotia, Canada, B2Z 1P8
Website: www.PottersfieldPress.com
To order, phone 1-800-NIMBUS9 (1-800-646-2879) www.nimbus.ns.ca

Printed in Canada

This book is dedicated
to all those who suffered
as a result of the crash
of Swissair 111

Like the Ancient Mariner
we tell our story
over and over again
hoping for relief
from the grief
that has inhabited us
for so long

# Contents

| | |
|---|---|
| Introduction | 9 |
| September 1, 1998 | 13 |
| The Start | 16 |
| Victims | 22 |
| Traffic | 28 |
| Stalled Business | 31 |
| Next Days | 33 |
| The Divers | 37 |
| Ordinary People | 40 |
| Families' Arrival | 41 |
| Dr. John Butt | 43 |
| Hotel Extraordinaire | 45 |
| Halifax | 48 |
| Nomenclature | 50 |
| Peggy's Cove | 51 |
| Golf Balls for Monte | 54 |
| The Bears | 56 |
| A Gift of Music | 57 |
| Claire | 61 |
| Nancy's Quilt | 63 |
| Lost Survivors | 65 |
| Commander Rick Town | 66 |
| Major John O'Donnell | 68 |
| The Morgue | 70 |

| | |
|---|---|
| Counsellors (I) | 77 |
| The Grapple | 78 |
| The Barge | 79 |
| The RCMP at East River | 80 |
| Judge Lorne Clarke | 83 |
| List | 85 |
| Poisoned Words | 86 |
| Epiphany | 87 |
| The Citadel Ceremony | 92 |
| Debra's Stones | 96 |
| Counsellors (II) | 98 |
| Connections | 104 |
| September 2015 | 109 |
| Acknowledgements | 112 |
| Appendix: One Year After the Crash | 119 |
| The Sea Change Quilt – Barb Robson | 121 |
| About the Author | 123 |
| Books by Budge Wilson | 125 |

# Introduction

At 10:31 on the night of September 2, 1998, Swissair Flight 111, en route from New York to Geneva, plunged into the sea a few kilometres beyond St. Margaret's Bay on the coast of Nova Scotia – close to Peggy's Cove on one side of the Bay, and to Bayswater and Blandford on the opposite shore.

From across Nova Scotia, vast numbers of emergency vehicles set off almost immediately from many locations – first to search for the precise location of the crash, then to set up rescue operations, and finally to accept the fact that there would be no one to rescue. The fractured remains of the 229 passengers and crew were gradually recovered by a valiant multitude of people, including fishermen, RCMP officers, military personnel, and many others. What was found was transported to a morgue at Shearwater to be identified. Led by Dr. John Butt, Chief Medical Officer of the Province of Nova Scotia, this enormous and complicated identification process took place with unusual efficiency, speed, and sensitivity.

However, the various recovery and identification operations took a huge toll on literally thousands of the people who were involved: the families and loved ones of the victims; those who operated the small and large boats that went out the first night and thereafter to bring back what they had hoped would be survivors; the divers who searched the dangerous floor of the ocean; those who watched from the fishing villages a few kilometres from the crash site; the many who comforted the bereaved; and the other dedicated people who participated in the whole heartbreaking experience. The impact of the tragedy reached far along Nova Scotia's shoreline, and has persisted.

This collection of poems is written in gratitude and in celebration of those thousands of men and women who suffered – and sometimes triumphed – during the months and years that followed the crash of Swissair Flight 111.

Those of us who were close to the disaster, whether through family or love or association; whether through involvement in the search and recovery, or in the subsequent comfort and care that was so badly needed; whether because of the accident of where we were and when it happened; or because of the simple fact of geography, we were changed forever by that terrible night in the air and on the sea. Some of this multitude will carry the intensity of their pain to the end of their days, without relief or true consolation. Others, although remembering with unremitting clarity the shock and the sorrow, the horror and the fear, have already learned surprising lessons about the possibilities of human courage and of love. They will, I hope, remember forever that ordinary flawed people are capable of a depth of kindness and generosity that is truly astonishing. And many of us have come to the stunning realization of the degree to which we all need one another.

I feel a unique gratitude to the families of the victims of the Swissair crash, who have permitted us to be a part of their pain. David and Janet Wilkins, father and mother of Monte, sat at our round kitchen table at Northwest Cove with Robert Conrad, my husband Alan, and me, in November of 2001. After five hours of talk and of listening – with each of us telling our own story – David said, "I never understood the whole picture until this afternoon." Then he turned to me and asked, "Do the sea and the wind sing for you again?"

"Yes," I replied, "they do."

I ask myself how a man, so torn and ravaged by his own large grief, could summon the generosity of spirit to care about my own small personal experience of loss. But he did, and I am the richer for it.

That significant act of unselfishness brought me closer to realizing that we all needed the families as much as they needed us. And in sharing memories of their loved ones, they gave substance and meaning to the faceless and formless grief that we had been feeling for so long. This has been no small gift, and we are grateful.

What follows is the story of what we saw, heard, and learned on September 2, 1998, and thereafter.

# September 1, 1998

Fog
and a smothering darkness
but out on Horse Island
the muttering voices of cormorants
   greeting the day
the tentative warm-up of engines
brief bursts of voices and laughter
   muffled but certain
the splash of an oar on the water
these are the sounds of the morning
before it begins

   The fog is so peaceful a thing
   unselfishly undemanding
   with its blurred lines
   its readiness just to be there
   its refusal to push any water
   into a shape or a size
   its patience

But soon
the briefest of wind
and the fog is dispersing
light struggles through
   catching a gull on the point
   and the white of the flagpole
the last boat has left
the hum of its motor far off
or only a memory

Day has begun

By ten o'clock they are back
the boats and the men
and a woman or two
the sounds on the wharves are louder
the comings and goings
and then at odd times in the day
a repeating performance

And as evening approaches
on the other side
of the large and magnificent Bay
the sun
is bursting its light onto Shut-In
that island mountain of granite
the tiny houses of Indian Harbour
  and five miles away
   at Peggy's Cove
the edge of the lighthouse

And still they move in
they move out
those vessels
in fairest of weather or foul
in and out of the coves and the harbours
till day is far spent
harvesting hundreds of mackerel
for feeding the tuna  those giants of fish
larding them up for the market
in faraway lands

This is a life that is hard
but in spite of
   the lifting of nets
   the hauling of oars in the wind
    as they circle the traps
   the pouring down of the weather
   the wet and the punishing cold
the people who've chosen to do this
possess a predictable rhythm
a knowing of peace that is centred
and with their work on the sea
a deep satisfaction

## The Start
Wednesday, 10:31 p.m. September 2, 1998

St Margaret's Bay
is wide
shaped like a horseshoe

On one side
Indian Harbour
Peggy's Cove
Dover

On the other
Aspotogan
Bayswater
Blandford

And out beyond the horseshoe's arms
at the wide serene horizon
over that space
came Swissair One Eleven
eight hundred feet up
six hundred and seventy-nine miles per hour
and plunged
nose down
into the sea

Many of us heard it
felt it

A silence followed
and the passage of time

Then
emergency vehicles came
hundreds of them
flares were dropped
boats set out
    from nearby fishing communities
    from Halifax
    from out at sea
    a small fleet of larger vessels
    a stark white cruise ship

The *Preserver* came
and stayed
(a heroic ship
that took what others found)

A lot of people live along those shores
what was it like
to witness all of this?

"We heard the plane," she said.
"It sounded wrong;
rattling
like six helicopters.
We turned off the TV
to listen.
It sounded wrong."

"The boom was far away," he said,
"and much like distant thunder";
(his house behind a hill that blocked the sea)
"I turned over then," he said,
"and slept till morning."

"The sound?  My God,
It felt as though ten tons
of weight
had landed on our house.
We ran outside
to look for damage,
but our roof was fine,
still there."

"Later, the flares came.
The Bay was like the battlefields
we've seen in films.
Wild,
but I got to admit
with a fearsome beauty."

"I wakened to the screaming
of sirens
and to light
ricocheting
off my bedroom wall.

"We're used to sirens here;
ambulances racing to heart attacks,
to accidents;
police cars rushing to break-ins,
to drunk drivers,
to stabbings;
(we have crime here, too, you know)
fire trucks shrieking along
to house fires,
to explosions,
to false alarms.

"We're used to all of that.

"But this,
this was different.

"Later  from the wharf I watched.
I didn't know
there could be that many
emergency vehicles
in the whole of Nova Scotia.
Lights flashing, revolving, glaring,
sirens wailing, cutting the air
like twisted knives,
from close by, from ten miles away,
still coming, coming.
Loudspeakers droning
with undecipherable messages,
the night alive with sound and blinding light."

Lorri
(who lived in Hubbards
and could see those vehicles
race down the shore road)
said,
"They looked like a string
of Christmas tree lights,
of moving Christmas lights,
stretching from our road
right down to Northwest Cove."

"Then we saw the fishermen,"
said one of the women,
"start up their engines,
leave their wharves,
set out to sea.
Marshall Boutilier with a boatful
of men in orange suits,
bright against the blackness
of the sea."

"Why? What is it? What happened?"

"Whatever it is," said Millie,
"it sure is big.
Some big."

Inside we turned on our TVs
and then we knew

CNN
that giant of networks
displaying a map
with four names only
Halifax  Peggy's Cove  Blandford  St. Margaret's Bay
not New York  Cincinnati  Los Angeles  Denver
no
our own place
and out beyond the Bay
an X
with the words
Swissair 111

## Victims

This was the night
that changed us

So many
so many
have suffered a sea change

The two hundred and twenty-nine
yes

The mourners
the families
the friends
all those
yes
weeping for loved ones
  sons  daughters
  lovers
  husbands and wives
  parents
  even babies  small babies
all of them
all
(except one  just one)
reduced to fragments
in one single
endless
moment

But more
so many  many more

Who were they?
those other thousands
  who cared
  who toiled
  who wept
  who became something new?

Something new
and often better
  giving
  daring
  sharing
oddly enriched
by a strange sense of completion
  but others
  those wounded veterans
  of that indelible night
  ravaged and torn
  by someone else's grief

These were the fishermen
pulled from their beds
with their wide-eyed sons
but full of hope
all of them
first on the water that black Wednesday
hearts high
racing out beyond Owl's Head
beyond Whale's Back

out  out to where the flares
would drop so soon
out between Peggy's Cove and Bayswater
out on the dark water
to pick up survivors

But that of course
is not what they would find

What they found
  has changed their lives
  inhabited their dreams
  bombarded them with images
  visions
  memories
  unwanted and unbidden

After that night
that Wednesday awful night
some told their stories to their wives
  their friends
  their counsellors
  their priests
  strangers on a bus
  to anyone who would listen

Most others wrapped up their pain
and buried it inside
keeping silent
mindful that men
strong men

must not cry
must not scream
must not be too weak or sick to work
for if they speak their horror and their fear
might not all those things happen?
might they not weep like babies
on the Government Wharf
with their friends there to see
brows knotted  whispering?

they cannot speak
their throats are seized shut
their children are watching
so are their wives
twisting their aprons

Better to say nothing
lest they weep

The next day  on Thursday morning
a man who found a broken child
washed up on the shore
(beside his lobster buoys
  his ropes  his rusting anchors)
let loose a primal scream
that echoes still
fades and returns
forever and forever
to those who heard
but now he cannot speak of it
the anguish has solidified
and he is mute

About that scream
its cadence branded ever in my ear
I will ask no questions
for I want no answers

Robert Conrad
from Fox Point
down the shore a piece
out in his boat to rescue survivors
found another child
thought he was a doll
lifted him from the water
tenderly wrapped him in a blanket
cradled him  loved him
and wept his grief
his rage
until the naval boats came
to empty the fishing vessels
of their appalling cargo

The small ship
that raced to the scene from Shelburne
its men fired up with excitement
with imagined heroics
the vision of saved lives
helicopters coming to transfer
the wounded
the joyful rescue
from the hungry sea
a tale to tell their children in front of the fire
toasting marshmallows over a dying flame
on a balmy August evening

And then at dawn
upon their arrival at the site
the shock of lost hope
and horror unthinkable
a scene upon which to shut one's eyes
smother one's voice

But you cannot shut your eyes
when what you now must do
is gather the dead
bring them on board
do what you are asked to do
muffle your heart maybe
lest it break
pretend there is an end to all of this

Later remember
wait
try to sleep at day's end
so many people weeping without tears
more often than not
alone

## Traffic

It was some rough out there
that night
15 to 20 foot waves
and it was dark
but not dead black
no  there was the flares
and lights from all the boats
our fishing vessels
and the green and red signals
from the Zodiacs
but right confusing
needing a lot of know-how with a boat
I think we did as good
as any navy boats could do
and there's some as say
better
it's not for me to say
such a thing
but the traffic sure was thick
and we had to keep those reds and greens
steady
as we wove ourselves
among ourselves and them
hauling what was left of plane and people
out of the sea
and no place to put them
no
except in our fish boxes
just fish boxes
I minded that some bad

And the lights
wavering and shimmering
off the high water
and the shoal nearby
with its waves wild white
in the darkness
seventeen years later
I remember it good

The paramedics
in their orange suits
could see right swift
there'd be no need for them
out there tonight
so Marshall took them back
they tried to pay him
but I heard him say
that no one would be looking
to be paid for anything
that night

He left them at the Government Wharf
but then went back
to get his son
to bring him home
far from that awful sea
no place for a young person
out there
best to leave the nightmares
for the older men

You get on with life
after such a thing
you has to
but yes  you're right
it troubles me some still
and there's those as has
black thoughts
near every night
and oftentimes
by day

# Stalled Business

I asked another fisherman

What about fishing?

It stopped  wasn't allowed
from Sambro to Lunenburg
we were shut out
the Fisheries people came
and closed up the entrance
to our traps
to our own fish
the mackerel were denied us
the tuna were hungry
but we weren't permitted to feed them

Then
when they finally let us do it
they came with us at feeding times
Department of Fisheries men  police
checking  making sure

I asked where they got the mackerel
for the tuna
when they couldn't catch them

Bought them  they said

Not a quick way  I thought  to make a living

To be locked out of a building
is hard
but for a fisherman to be barred
from entrance to the sea
must be frustrating beyond belief
a constraint unthinkable

I heard no complaints

# Next Days

The army people arrive
most of them young
some of them women
three hundred and fifty strong
living in a tent city in Blandford
combing the beaches
moving aside the shells  the kelp  the driftwood
searching between the granite rocks
eyes down
silent (no laughter here
no quips
no smiles)
looking  looking
armed with their bags
their shovels
their long forks
searching for what they do not wish to find

The Zodiacs too
moving slowly
without sound
up and down the shores
of St. Margaret's Bay and beyond
and among the islands
(three hundred and more of them)
keeping close to the tide line
their black-clad divers
in and out of the water
like slippery seals
not speaking

pieces of plane
pieces of people
a shoe
a scrap of metal
a five-dollar bill
remnants

A young woman
Cynthia
a single parent
short of cash
with urgent messages on her e-mail
no time to spare
sees a group of soldiers searching her little beach

She is a quick cook
she knows how
makes two dozen muffins
   and takes them down to the soldiers
she does this often
she says she will never again
make a muffin
without seeing Flight 111
in the flour  the milk  the baking powder

In the meantime
week after week
a large army of women
from Seabright to Peggy's Cove
from Fox Point to East River
bakes up a storm
Nanaimo bars  chocolate squares  donuts

macaroons  banana cream pies  TREATS
delivered to the tent city and to the trailers
  at Indian Harbour
  Peggy's Cove
  East River
  Blandford
to wherever there are workers to encourage
to thank

In Blandford
at the tent city
a freezer as large as a dumpster
(I saw it)
filled to the sides and top
with their gifts
cooked with love
  or gratitude
  or admiration
  or anguish
while in the close background
the constant cacophonous rattle
of helicopters
is squeezing their nerves tight
with an ongoing pressure
but still
baking and giving

And later
after the families come
  women comforting loved ones
  helping and holding them
  hearing their stories

keeping the tea hot
quick with a meal
a bed
or a Kleenex

They are all there  these people
thousands of them

# The Divers

The deep-sea divers
these are among the most heroic
we find it hard to even think of them

They are ordinary men
they have wives and lovers
  children
  mortgages
  fears
  longings
  difficult angers

They test their gear
  the valves
  the lifelines
  the suit fastenings
  their goggles
keeping their minds as empty as caves

Don't think
refuse entry to panic and horror
with their hundred different faces
forget what's down there
what you saw yesterday
what you may meet today

Just do your job

They are lowered into the water

Be careful
your lifeline is your life
do not rip your suit
don't think
be careful

You go down  down from the bright sea surface
down  down two hundred long feet
where it is dark and
dangerous
dark
dangerous
and full of tenacious images
you work among the wreckage
among plane fragments
as sharp as razor blades
as lethal
you work among the dead
unrecognizable
caught by seat belts
by rocks
by sand

What was once the nose of the plane
is where you are
so is the tail
and all that lies between

From the sea bottom
   the wreckage rises nineteen feet
and stretches as long and as wide
as two football fields

If the nose is where the tail is
what does that mean?
don't think
just do your job
but be careful
one diver has already almost died
not you
not yet

Do your job
don't think
bring up the people first
the almost people
rescuing the plane comes later

Be careful

## Ordinary People

Those of us who live beside the shore
view the large vessels
notice how low the helicopters are flying
see the circling gulls
watch the army trucks thundering along the road
go down to the wharf each morning
(as instructed)
to scan
to inspect the tide line
observe the surface of the water

are alert for what we may see
what we may find

Here is the number to call
if you find anything

What do you mean  anything?

Anything unusual
call us
don't touch anything

Anything?

Well  we're not talking about driftwood
old lobster pots
stray buoys

Call us
we'll decide

## Families' Arrival

On Friday and Saturday
the families start to arrive
hundreds of them

they move slowly
clinging to one another
there is not much to hear
the falling of tears is not a noisy sound

They stream into the Lord Nelson Hotel
in Halifax
where warm arms reach out
  to comfort
  to assist
  to transport
  to listen

Some are refusing to abandon
a futile hope
but most have come to mourn
and to accompany the bodies of their loved ones
home
for proper burial
it will be hard
so hard
but there will be some sort of narrowing
of that vast gaping circle of grief

Later they gather in the area
up the stairs from the lobby
in what used to be
a high and gracious reception room
now it is theirs
it will belong to them
for many days and weeks to come
    for new arrivals
    for meetings and announcements
    for messages
    for being with one another

Today they assemble in the auditorium
to hear what Dr. John Butt has to say to them
he is the Chief Medical Officer
    of the Province of Nova Scotia
he is admired for his objectivity
his cool efficiency
his self-control under pressure
he oversees the morgue at Shearwater
where it is assumed
they will go
to identify the bodies
of their loved ones

Sharing their communal torment
they wait for his arrival

# Dr. John Butt

In his work  John Butt
has stayed aloof
from the families
of the dead
this has worked best for him

He stands now
before the people  the mourners
their eyes are on him
lost eyes
hundreds of them
awaiting his message

His message is a terrible one
but he has delivered terrible messages before
and then gone home to eat his dinner
walk his dogs
and admire the view from his veranda

This time is different
who can say why?
no dead  surely  are more dead than others
no set of mourners more stunned by grief

His objectivity deserts him
his self-control staggers
his heart  much larger than he had ever imagined
is wide open

When he tells them that
no  there are no survivors
few are surprised
they have read the newspapers
watched the television

But now he has to tell them
that they cannot come
  to identify their loved ones
that they cannot take
their bodies home for burial
that out of two hundred and twenty-nine people
only one
just one
has been found intact

This he does
he tells them all of that
and weeps publicly
for them
and with them
without shame

John Butt has just gone through a door
he didn't know was there
and on the other side
he steps into an area of tears
but full of light

# Hotel Extraordinaire

The Lord Nelson Hotel
strategically located
opposite the Halifax Public Gardens
  a peaceful and beautiful place
  in which to walk and to grieve
close to restaurants and shops
and the normal comings and goings
of Haligonians
this was the hotel of choice
for housing the mourners

Under new management
with a lot of renovation underway
in a busy state of transition
the hotel was nevertheless
willing and glad to receive them

The residents  knowing these plans
were told they were free to stay
or to go
but most departed
leaving the hotel as the temporary home
for a host of broken-hearted people

The large and gracious Regency Room
set aside as their space
was arranged with coffee at the ready
chairs  tables  snacks
stations of common communication
for sad but crucial discussion

this place was theirs
for many weeks
for as long as the need was there

In the individual rooms
there were messages of condolence
of empathy
flowers
a welcome

The staff were told
they might mingle with the guests
or not  as they saw fit
not an easy
not a simple thing to do
but desire was there to diminish the anguish
if only a little

Lesa
who worked in the Sales office
knew that she wanted to help
but feared to speak to the mourners
loath to intrude on their sorrow
but approaching a man
who was standing alone
she spoke

"May I help you in any way?"
she asked  dreading his answer
but he said  "Please
I'd like you to sit down with me somewhere
and hold my hand"
which she did

Lesa came down to the Regency Room each
morning
and there he was
every day
waiting

No one said to Lesa
"It's time to get back to work"
no
the people who ran that hotel
managers  owners
allowed and encouraged
the links between staff and their grieving guests
who remember this still

And afterwards
when nightmares occurred
and a surfeit of memories
of such a concentration of pain
counsellors were brought in
to assist the troubled in spirit
the caring  compassionate staff

Sixteen years later
When Lesa told me the story
of the man whose hand she held
there were tears in her voice

The Lord Nelson Hotel
a hotel with a very big heart

# Halifax

Halifax
city of wars  of rum-runners
of small and enormous disasters
of quiet hospitality
with its massive Citadel
its famous harbour  with its graceful bridges
its sumptuous dwellings
its flat-faced houses  flush with the sidewalk
this city of trees
it was here that the mourners would come

On the first night
of their arrival in Halifax
the parents
the sons and the daughters
the fiancés  scores of the loved ones
wandered Spring Garden Road
searching for restaurants
for their late evening meal
  but most were closed
  stoves were cooling
  lights were dimming
the restaurant day was over

But seeing the name tags on their jackets
restaurant after restaurant
opened its doors
took down its CLOSED sign
heated up the stoves
and fed them

And there were also more than a few
who refused to accept any money

And many Haligonians
aware of their suffering
   their sense of such deep alienation
invited them into their homes
offering whatever they could
a bed  a chair at their table
to ease such an excess of sorrow

Members of Delta Alliance
who arrive after airline disasters
   to assess  to assist
set up their offices
close to the Lord Nelson Hotel

And in wonder  they said of our city
old  shabby  beloved
that they'd never witnessed before
not ever before
such a warm outpouring of kindness
such a generous spirit of giving
as they saw unfolding before them
in the city of Halifax

# Nomenclature

Nomenclature:

*The families* come to mean
    all the mourners who travel from afar.
*The first night* or just *that night* is synonymous
    with Wednesday night, September 2nd,
    and for many months,
    for years in fact,
    means the time of the crash, the disaster.
*Our crash:* We feel that it is ours,
    and that sense of ownership
    affects us deeply.
*Friday* refers to the day the families start to arrive.
*Swissair* becomes the short form
    for The Swissair Flight 111 Crash. People say:
    *After Swissair I was depressed for weeks;*
    *People's barriers were lowered after Swissair;*
    *Swissair is now part of my emotional history.*

We use these terms still,
    seventeen [or whatever] years later.

Just say to me, *That night,*
and the whole experience appears before me,
fully formed,
in colour
and wired for sound.

## Peggy's Cove

On Saturday and thereafter
the families
travel by bus
by car
to Peggy's Cove
Peggy's Cove becomes for a time
indeed for a long time
probably still
even now
a kind of shrine for the mourners.

The village is roped off
from traffic
from the curious

For over a week the families
own the lighthouse
the enormous rocks
they cling to the people who live there
drink their tea
tell them their stories
weep at their kitchen tables
they sit or stand on the rocks
arms around one another
facing the horizon
their personal graveyard
some throw flowers into the sea
or teddy bears for the children

On TV we see a soldier
or maybe he's a bus driver
(he has a uniform on)
he's crouched behind a giant rock
crying

From the other shore
the Aspotogan shore
five miles away
we see the figures on the rocks
through our binoculars
they look like
tragic insects
black against the white granite
not moving

One day the sea
is too turbulent
to let the families
go close to the water
the RCMP won't permit it
but firefighters form a human chain
down to the water

From a barrier
a mourner hands a rose to an RCMP man
    and says a name
he passes the name and flower to a fireman
and another and another

The last man
tethered to a rope
that can rescue him from a rogue wave
repeats the name
pauses
and tosses the rose into the heaving sea

Another memento  another name
is passed down the line
and is joined to the waves

Again and again this happens

Only the Wilkins family
mourning Monte
aged nineteen
changes the rhythm
by standing on the rocks
and singing "It Is Well With My Soul"
and
"Amazing Grace"

Nobody there will soon forget
that day

## Golf Balls for Monte

So
sure
they threw their flowers
into the sea
like everyone else
but for them
the singing was good
the throwing was not
not entirely fitting  not exactly appropriate
for Monte
no

So what should they do?
what was his passion  his delight?

Golf
yes

A policewoman gave them a golf club  a driver
the balls were provided  who knows from where

They gathered themselves
  their friends
  their equipment
near the old cemetery  close to the beach
and there
on a brisk fall day
as only Nova Scotia knows how to make them
sunny and clear
with an offshore wind
their hearts in a state
of odd inexact satisfaction

David and Darren drove ball after ball
into the ocean
until they were all gone

It wasn't what you could call
a happy golf game
but it felt right

In 1999  one year later
Robert Conrad would take the whole family
  and Nancy Wight
out in his boat
and they would drop the club into the sea
at the exact spot
where the plane had entered

Monte's identified remains
are buried in a small cemetery
in Blandford

Over the years
I've kept golf balls in my car
and sometimes
when passing the graveyard
I leave a ball in the grass
beside his stone

It's never alone
others have come before me
to leave behind the same strange flower

## The Bears

The Red Cross
distributed teddy bears
(gifted by Zellers and The Bay)
among the family members

On Halifax streets  at Peggy's Cove  at Shearwater
adults could be seen carrying around those bears
holding them close

Somebody knew
(somebody smart)
that it can be helpful
in some basic way
to have something to hug

# A Gift of Music

On the sharp edge of all the sorrow
came Dawn Upshaw
African Nova Scotian
living in Halifax  born in Three Mile Plains

Feeling the sharpness  knowing the heartache
hearing the words of an African mourner
whose sister and two little daughters
   had died in the crash
she longed to ease some of the pain
to acknowledge the suffering

Dawn went to her father and asked
"What can I do to help?"
"Follow your heart" he replied

She did

She thought to gather together
six members of her community
to travel to Peggy's Cove
to sing  to comfort  to strengthen  to thank
the families and workers

She lifted her phone  with its unlisted number
and started her search for a van
to transport her friends
on their musical journey
their mission of song

So deep are the spiritual links
of the Black community
that like a warm and urgent wind
sweeping across the province
from Yarmouth to Sydney Mines
from church to church
from village to town
from e-mails to telephones
from voices over the fences
came the messages

"We want to come"

"We need to be there"

Metro Transit offered a bus
then two
three  then four
the bus drivers drove free of charge
Forbes Chev-Olds lent three vans

And still the phone  with its unlisted number
continued to ring and to ring
as Dawn contrived to cut through
the red tape and government protocol
to permit their entry
to allow their loving invasion
of the restricted Peggy's Cove site

The next day was sunless and grey
with a driving wind and a turbulent sea
and before very long
they started to come
in cars and in vans and in four Metro buses
from Digby  Acaciaville  LeQuille  and Middleton
from Antigonish  Glace Bay  Lincolnville  Mulgrave
and Truro  Springhill  and North and East Preston
from Halifax and thirty-seven other communities
they arrived and arrived
until three hundred and fifty people
grouped at the foot of the Peggy's Cove lighthouse
to offer their music  their voices
their massive compassion

They dressed in and with colour
to lift and to celebrate spirit
the people of Peggy's Cove
brought snacks and hot and cold drinks
as did the singers
completing the traditional African bond
of food and music and prayer

From early to late afternoon
they came and they sang
piercing the dimness of the day
with the bright light of their music

They sang for the victims  the mourners
for the weary and haunted fishermen
the troubled retrievers
the RCMP and the Coast Guard Auxiliary

the Canadian Forces  armed only with mercy
the police and the firefighters
for those who were present
and those who were no longer there

Their spirituals  their musical prayers
as familiar as breath to the singers
embraced the listeners
with a palpable love
a giving of strength  of audible comfort
Of such was their warmth
their giving of spirit
their spirit of giving

    Some gestures  some people or events
    can face a rushing river of despair
    and at least for a time
    still its wild waters

    Dawn Upshaw and her caring community
    caused this to happen

Five days later
at Province House in the City of Halifax
the Members of the Legislative Assembly
of the Province of Nova Scotia
rose
and thanked her

# Claire

During the gathering at Indian Harbour
six days after the crash
with families  with loved ones
with local people  children singing
with international dignitaries
  and the watchful media
with weary workers of all kinds
beside the microphones
  the flags
  the boxes of Kleenex
after the music
  the speeches
  the prayers
  the long and sombre reading of the names
there came a pause

Onto the stage stepped Claire Mortimer
  unplanned
  unannounced
  unexpected
her long hair and long skirt
moving in the wind
she held the microphone
and in a voice both soft and steady
spoke

What she said was
a thank you
to our country and the province of Nova Scotia
(with special poignant mention of the fishermen)

These gifts of hospitality and help
(she told us)
had not gone unnoticed
would not be forgotten

Nor have her quiet  grateful words

She was the first
we heard say them

Around the shores of St. Margaret's Bay
on wharves  in kitchens
at gas stations  on chip wagons
few do not know her name

Thank you  Claire  for that bright steady candle
lit with love
for our own darkness

# Nancy's Quilt

Listen to this

Alone  but for her daughter
(beautiful  talented)
she lived her life

The plane came down
and took her daughter with it

Can we imagine such pain?
no  I think not
can we give her the comfort that will heal her?
no  I fear not

She was brave
she went to a quilt show
liked quilts
your heart can be torn to shreds
but you can still
love quilts

Later
led by Barb Robson
seventy-three women made
seventy-five blocks
in patterns of stars
twenty-five women did
the quilting

The backing was a rose pattern
at first they'd called it
"Celestial Rose"
But "Rows" was the nickname
of her daughter  Rowenna
they changed the name
to "Celestial Rows"
and gave it to Nancy
a gift of astonishing love

Something more
a mystery

Those ninety-eight women
needed to make that quilt
as much as she needed to receive it

# Lost Survivors

At the Lord Nelson in Halifax
at Peggy's Cove  at Blandford
in a strange land  in vacant rooms  in kitchens
(grasping their hot tea  boiled tea  strong)
crazed or stunned by grief
or weeping  weeping
the families  the loved ones
needing  needing

# Commander Rick Town

This crash spawned many heroes
unknown  unheralded
the list is long
of people without names
or even faces

Bow your heads
give thanks
place your admiration at their feet
and be amazed

But one man
(it seems to me)
was close to the peak of that vast pyramid of caring

Commander Rick Town
stood on his ship
HMCS *Preserver*
and held the world together
with his voice
calm and caring
sending out messages to the smaller vessels
to the retrievers
making it possible for them
to live for a time
in a floating hell
with his voice
strong and compassionate
leading  directing  informing
preventing hysteria

stilling the screams that tore at their throats
making it possible
    to stay
    and to do it

While on his own ship
knowing the limits
of human endurance
observing his crew
watching their eyes
their ways of bending  of lifting
alert to the signs
of the folding  the breakage
of human spirits

And all the long hours
ignoring his own
deep fractures

If I live long enough
I pray
that I may some day
meet this man

# Major John O'Donnell

Major John O'Donnell
friend to us all
Chaplain to more than the military
whose eyes were open
to the needs of all people
and where he saw needs
he followed
moving into the place
they existed
   to offer solutions
   deliver compassion
   to pray or to counsel

From the very beginning  John did this
from the moment he joined the mourners
at the Lord Nelson Hotel
he could see that
   their way of standing
   their faces  their restless hands
   or the fact of being alone
could reveal the extent of their need

By a question  suggestion
an offer of help
or a touch
he brought warmth and support
to the frightened  the lonely
and to those rendered numb by their grief

This is a man who knew how
to join people to people

At Peggy's Cove
where they gathered
to honour their loved ones
by throwing flowers into the sea
he choreographed the sad dance
ever alert
to the special beliefs and responses
  of individuals
  of groups
he stood with them all on the rocks
and as much as is possible
felt what they felt

And as time  short and long
passed by
attending or leading memorial services
  week after week
  and eventually
  year after year
    at Indian Harbour
    at the Basilica  at Whale's Back
    at Bayswater
    at the Halifax Citadel
and often in kitchens or hallways
or maybe on somebody's wharf
with a congregation of one

We all of us
thank John O'Donnell
for leaving the scene of Swissair
a warmer  more merciful place

# The Morgue

I am Bart
I worked at the Shearwater morgue

I was twenty-two years old
in the army
in the Medical Corps
someday I will be a doctor

Because the civic authorities
weren't ready
with equipment or people
to do the job
we were asked
or told
to do it

We did

We thought we'd seen everything
we hadn't
we thought we'd be strong
that for us
(accustomed to death and mutilation)
this would not be so very difficult
not easy
but O.K.
manageable

It was not

Shearwater
the Shearwater morgue
became
yes  it did
my home

On the very next day
we started
(twenty of us)
twelve hours a day
shutting our minds off
we did it

No  I didn't mind so much
I'd go home at night
my folks were there
quite easy  really

The authorities forbade us
to look at the belongings
the wallets full of cash
the passports
the photos
the postcards
(addressed  ready for mailing)
the Adidas  the sandals
(seldom matching)
the makeup cases
(lipstick  aspirin  Gravol for airsickness)
they kept those things from us
so that we could avoid realizing
that what we were working with
had once been
people

Maybe a good idea
and maybe not
so it was a deprivation
but perhaps a salvation

The one day when we broke down
was when
we opened a body bag
(so many body bags
so many)
to find
a little child

But we could not see the families
(so close by
in another hangar
identifying objects
belongings
weeping)
so we felt as though we were
not a part of
not connected to
this tragedy
empty
in a time
that was frozen
that did not move

Mostly we dealt with pieces
parts
nothing whole
how could we feel
a belonging?

The others
outside our hangar
read newspapers
saw TV
attended memorial services
hugged brothers
mothers
sons
baked cookies
wept with one another

They were there

We who were closest
were farthest away

We didn't go to Peggy's Cove
to the memorial sites
to Whale's Back
to Bayswater
we felt as though we'd be intruding
that we didn't belong

No  no
don't worry
we were fine

We were not fine
not at all
I couldn't sleep
I would get up and drive to someone's home
a friend who had no family to return to
who was sitting up in the dark
alone

Then we would be together
this was better
than staring into the dark
eyes wide open
eyes too full for closing
we didn't like dark places
the freezer was dark

One night I drove
away from the morgue
taking half the parking lot with me
right through the rope enclosure
dragging everything after me
that tired
that crazed

But we needed to go back
needed to finish the job
needed to have it done
and then
return to who we used to be
regain the selves
that we had put on hold

One day the civic authorities arrived
said
now we're ready
now you can leave
we can complete the work

We all  all
felt orphaned
homeless
our job undone
our closure denied us

When  how  could I return
to my self
to whom I once had been
now that our mission
had been interrupted
stolen

I felt like those dead people
on a journey
with the destination
removed
I felt like the families
waiting for their loved ones
as I await the return
of my self
but they did not arrive
nor did I

And this grieves and frightens me

I had planned to be a cardiologist
or a plastic surgeon

Not now

I will be a field doctor
probably no wife or family
(this seems irrelevant
at the moment)
probably with little money
(for things I do not need)
I will go where there are land mines
where people are torn and broken
and try to mend them

# Counsellors (I)

How to be a counsellor
at that time
(and there were many)

How to sit there
(eyes careful  lest they tell their own story)
and listen

How to hear what you have heard
(stockpiling images)
and then
find the strength
to return home  hang up your car keys
pretend to eat your dinner
read bedtime stories to your kids
help wash the dishes
try to explain why lovemaking is impossible

Lie awake till dawn

# The Grapple

The *Grapple* came
from the U.S.
a large and vicious-seeming ship
with hoists and metal arms
a tangle of groping steel
with cages to lower the divers
to bring up what remained
of Swissair 111
pieces of plane
pieces of people
day after day
week after week

We could see it from the shore
an enormous sinister insect
searching for prey

## The Barge

Those who have seen the barge
will not forget it

Moving so slowly
up and down the Bay
a vessel dark and ominous and low
at dusk
travelling without sound
(no engines heard)
away from the *Grapple*
into the Bay
something to see
while having
a cheerful gin and tonic
on the wharf
no laughter now
a silence falls
a scene to place
the darkest cloud of knowing
onto the brightest day

Take your terrible cargo
into the shore
and let night fall

## The RCMP at East River

We are the RCMP
Two hundred strong

We camp out in trailers
at East River
using the Union Hall
   for eating
   for talking
   for sitting in silence

Around the clock
we work in shifts
   all night
   all day

The trucks come
drive us ten miles
to New Harbour
we board the small vessels
in the cold dawn
or maybe in the dark and clutching night
out over the sea
to the west of Ironbound Island
to the *Grapple*
our minds numb
bodies tense

And there we stay until our shift is done

Our job is sorting
sorting what the divers
have brought up for us
from the sea's wounded and lacerated floor

Do it
try to keep your mind neutral
blank
look (because you must
it's part of the job)
but try to let what you see
bypass your brain
try to prevent that lump that chokes your throat
from spilling over
into something unmanageable

After a stretch
of long immeasurable time
the endless shift is over

Dazed
relieved
we start the journey
to what has become our dwelling place
into the Zodiacs
over the sea
past Pearl Island
(such a clean and lovely name)
to New Harbour
go through the decontamination routine
pile into the trucks
drive the ten miles
to East River

Incredibly we're hungry
and we know there will be food
waiting for us
but
we hope the women have sent in
some special things
a layer cake  or pies  some chocolate squares
we need to know they know
and want to tell us
we need to feel their warm hands
on the small of our backs
knowing
thanking

# Judge Lorne Clarke

Mr. Justice Lorne Clarke
gentle of men
even and careful of temper and outlook
ready to explore
to examine
twenty-five different perspectives
thirty opinions
and countless hotly contested beliefs
without flying apart at the seams

Just as well

The Government of Nova Scotia
requested that Judge Clarke be the Chair
of the Memorial Advisory Committee
to choose the site for a fitting Memorial
or maybe two
and to make decisions about
the burial of all the unidentified remains

And Lorne Clarke agreed to the task
without payment
refusing a vote in the process
asking only
for an easily accessible parking space

It was not the simplest of mandates
but he approached it
as in all things
with humility and respect

with a rare and significant wisdom
not easily measured
and possibly  best of all
with a quiet and comfortable kindness

# List

A cacophony of images and sounds

The entry  the thundering death
the sirens  lights  the flares
the orange suits in Marshall's boat
the fishing vessels racing out to sea
the stories the next day
and next and next
Robert and the baby and his grief
(two Roberts)
the fish boxes
the gulls
the primal scream
black insects on the rocks across the Bay
and then the endless search

Endless
being the entirely accurate word

## Poisoned Words

I thought to try to read
to ease my mind
to take myself away from what I saw
outside my window
and inside my head

Magazine articles
short stories  comics
novels and poems
anything
try anything

But for a time
words dislodged themselves
from off the pages
left the solid text
and appeared before me
disembodied and alone

Words like
pieces  cut  sink
fall  sorrow  fear
down  find  lift
flashing  black  orange
water  fuel  body
search  broken  weep

The list is without end
a single page
could hold a dozen

No escape

# Epiphany

And so the darkness came to me
quite soon
even on sunlit days
the sea was grey
for me
the sea
so loved by me
so loved
was veiled
blurred by grief
inhabited by death
my eyes observed the beauty
felt it not
only the loss
I saw the images
and heard the scream
baked brownies for the RCMP
two and a half dozen each time
for two hundred men

The wind
so loved by me
so loved
listening to it like music
in the night
feeling it on my face
a blessing

The wind began to sing
another song
a song of fear

its lyrics somber  grim
a threatening sound
with messages of dread

So hard to sleep
to be at peace
I knew I needed help

From whom?

One thing came first
Robert Conrad
(that same fisherman who held the baby)
said
(knowing the love that bloomed along that shore)
"Peggy's Point and Aspotogan Point"
(which held the vast horizon in between)
"look to me like arms embracing"

He did not say
"embracing with comfort and love"
but that is what he meant

That helped

But still the horizon spoke
so sadly to me
so much of dark foreboding in that space

Do you not see how deep the knife had cut?

I said to Sister Dorothy Moore
sixteen long months later
"I want this thing to go away"

Her words to me were quiet
but so firm
"This thing" she said
"is not going to go away"

"Well then" I asked
"what now?"

"Think good things about the sea"
she said
"Pray"

I could scarcely believe
that her reply
would be so simple

Odd
I was disappointed
flat

But I who pray regularly
to St. Anthony
to find my car keys
and to God
about all manner of things
had never thought to pray
(not once)
for this

The next day
the very next day
I drove to Halifax
by the Shore Road
beside the beaches
the day was brilliant blue
with dazzling light
a January sun  low in the sky
in early morning
with a powerful wind
straight onshore

At Whynacht's Beach I stopped the car
looked directly
into the waves

The waves were huge
cresting
curling
their underbellies full of sun and gold
their pounding on the sand a giant heartbeat
the surface of the sea was breathing  breathing
with a luminous silver skin
and on the horizon
a dense and dancing band
of a million sun-struck diamonds

I watched and saw such beauty
as could make me cry

And yes  out on that band of diamonds
was Swissair
there with the radiance
with the silver skin
there with the loveliest sea
I'd ever seen
created by wind  my wind
sorrow and beauty wedded in one place

The sea received them
as gently as it could
it did not kill them

This is the gift God gave to me
that day

## The Citadel Ceremony
September 2, 1999

They came in hundreds
to the last farewell
of that first year

The Citadel was dark that night
as people climbed the hill
the air clear
and warm

At the top
buses let off their passengers
the families
here for the final ceremony
of September the second
1999
exactly one year later

Over the moat and beyond it
on the rough ground inside the fort
the people gathered
the families in front of the stage
on chairs
the rest of us grouped behind them and around
enclosed by the stark stone walls
beneath the ramparts

The ceremony
was much as you might expect
prayers  speeches
representatives of religious groups
the government
retrieval personnel
the Navy
the Coast Guard and Auxiliary
military workers
the RCMP
there were blessings and declarations
expressions of grief and of gratitude
tears
embraces

Throughout the evening
at intervals
musicians hallowed the scene
high on the fort's ledges
bright in the black night
singing their songs
of comfort and of grief

At exactly 10:31
a ship's bell rang
and all were silent
remembering

Beyond the silence of the Citadel's walls
Fifty churches rang their bells
cutting through the noise and clamour
of the city

And inside the fort
all of us together
quiet
needing one another
on that dark and troubled night

Then the procession started
of mourners and helpers
carrying their candles to the edge of the stage
slowly and carefully
hands unsteady
placing them there
a necklace of flickering light

Finally the bagpipes
played "MacGregor's Lament"
long and sad and powerful
its tempo slow and stately

Then
little by little
the pace quickened
the pipers' kilts
swaying with the change
and on the eastern parapet
far up
floodlit now against the darkness
the fiddlers started
with strong insistent beat

And to our wide astonishment
yes  and our shock
. but also with our deepest of relief
we heard a reel
music designed for dancing

And so we reached
the end of this first year
our earnest salutation
to the dead
and now
on this same night
our celebration
of the living

# Debra's Stones

Look at the beach
there on the sand is Debra
picking up stones
all shaped like hearts
perfect ones  crooked ones
the palest of grey
and smooth

Day after day she goes
back and forth  back and forth
collecting her hearts

A few children join her
and then
with her mother and neighbouring friends
they paint patterns and pictures
on the stones
a medley of chaotic colour and delight
but it is Debra  a true artist
who decorates most of them
and they are simple  delicate  rare

On the night before the seventh anniversary
of Swissair
when many are expected to arrive
to commemorate the crash
she lays 229 of her stones
along the edge of the granite base
of the Bayswater Memorial
where the floor meets the grass
that covers the unidentified remains
of the 229 victims

# plum™ rewards

| Points Required | Reward Value |
| --- | --- |
| 2,500 | $5 |
| 4,500 | $10 |
| 8,500 | $20 |
| 20,000 | $50 |
| 35,000 | $100 |

Explore the benefits of plum rewards and become a member for free! Visit indigo.ca/plumrewards to learn more.

Chapters **!ndigo** COLES indigo.ca

# plum™ rewards

| Points Required | Reward Value |
| --- | --- |
| 2,500 | $5 |

In case you need to return it.

Store# 00793 Term# 002 Trans# 646068
Operator: 886CM     06/17/2016 15:04

**GIFT RECEIPT**

*****************************************
-TER SWISSAIR                      BJJK
781897426814

*****************************************
**A GIFT FOR YOU**
*****************************************

Store# 00793 Term# 002 Trans# 646068

GST Registration # R897152666

*007930020640682*

Overnight
thirty of the stones are removed
but she checks the scene
before the ceremony begins
and without rancour or panic
returns to her home
and brings back thirty more
to complete her gift

It is intended that any people who want a stone
may take one
to remember
to hold in their hands

This they do
following the ceremony

This disaster  this tragedy
generated so much
    of fear and of sorrow
    of grief and of pain
that we should all rise
and thank Debra
    for her hearts
    for her heart
    for adding a note of love
    and of generous joy
    to a sad symphony

I have my stone still
kept in a special place

*(Incredibly, Debra created the same gift for the 10th anniversary)*

# Counsellors (II)

We are the counsellors

We came from all over
the need so huge

We talked with those
who thought it weak to talk
impossible  unthinkable to cry
   and heard them talk
   saw them cry

Who were those people whose tales we heard?

The families and loved ones  of course
their sorrow unbounded  rage without limit
their helpers  drivers  friends
(undone by such a deep infectious grief)

The searchers
   eyes focused downwards
   among the rocks  beneath the seaweed strands
   sifting  searching and finding
   a shoe a crucifix  a passport  a hand
   half buried in the sand
   wedged between granite boulders

The crews of helicopters
   flying low
   watching the grass
   flattening beneath the blades

ruffling the sea's surface
clattering the air into deafness
seeing too much

The RCMP
 the sorters
 cold and contaminated
 who travelled to the *Grapple*
 who loaded the barge
 grouping  arranging
 horror their bedfellows
 to witness  to hide  to reveal

The Coast Guard Auxiliary
 bombarded by phone calls
 longing for sleep
 with the constant preparing of food
 repairing of engines
 and begging for boats
 enduring  ignoring fatigue

The sea people
 fishermen and sailors
 women and men
 touching and lifting
 shocked into silence
 or weeping aloud

And media people
 did they come too?
 media people?  the vultures
 who fill the sound waves and the presses

with cruel events
who move in on death
with hungry microphones
and tape recorders
whose lifeblood is drawn from disasters?

The media people?
  yes
  they came to us too
  radio and TV crews
  their gear still strapped to their shoulders
  the reporters
  cell phones poised  pencils scratching
  came to us

They knew and saw it all
  on the spot
  at the scene

  First at the Government Wharf
  in Northwest Cove
  then on the beach at Bayswater
  and next on the water
  or setting up cameras and microphones
  at Peggy's Cove
  surrounded by
  scores of noisy flashing emergency vehicles
  the running to and fro of rescue workers
  the eerie red glow hitting the lowest clouds
  Armageddon  war  spiritual blindness  shell shock
  Drama  yes  and a stuttering hope
  hospitals alerted  beds waiting
  plasma at the ready

They knew all this

You think our media people
were greedy for horrors?

Think again

The rocks at Peggy's Cove are often chilly
even in the midsummer sun

In the black of that September night
and in the awful dawn
they were cold as death
and unforgiving

They watched
as the fishermen returned from their forays
    their eyes staring  hollow
They heard in the darkness
    "I cannot go out there again"
and gradually
    terrible graphic descriptions
    of the sea's unwilling new harvest
    the imagined scent of death in the air
    of spirits moving above the water

No
our own media were not so much hungry for details
    as stunned by them
    knowing compassion  shock
    and a fading hope

Not only did our camera crews show few pictures
most took no pictures
    sensing the sacredness of what they witnessed
    sparing the families
    sparing the readers
    sparing the watchers
    unable to spare themselves

And yes  the media came to us
in our makeshift offices
for the recurring images that came and went
unbidden
their odd feelings of guilt
their insomnia  their nighttime and daytime dreams
their clinging sadness

They had felt the shifting sands
beneath the rocks of Peggy's Cove
and would not ever again
be exactly the same people

And now
    there are therapists counselling therapists
    for if you've heard
    a thousand nightmare tales
    your head is crammed with
    pictures and with facts
    that steal your sleep
    invade your homes
    and block your eyes
    from peaceful closing

These
all these and more
are the throngs of damaged people
we have seen

We see them still

# Connections

Two decades will soon have passed
but still
yes  still our minds
are playing evil games
so that hearing one small word
or maybe just a sound
can take us back
to where it all began

I've wakened in my sleep
and seen that wet arena
the wounding of the spirit on that night
of those who walked the surfaces of hell

I've seen the men returning to the shore
dumb with a surfeit of seeing  of retrieving
mute to their wives (arms open  not receiving)
the men comfortless  vacant and grey of face
eyes crammed with pictures
I walk into their heads
and think their masked and scavenged thoughts

I hear them say things they do not mean and do
"Fine.  Oh sure, I'm fine.
Goddamnit does the baby have to cry so loud?
No breakfast.  No.  No food.  My God not bacon.
Coffee maybe.  Strong.  Can't you shut up that baby?
Give me some peace.
No.  It's okay.  There's nothing to tell.
Just leave me be.

I want to shut my eyes."
Nothing to tell
except the things that rip his gut
and stun his brain
and leave him with a lifetime of technicolour
nightmares
red the predominant colour
and eyes that cannot shut
against what he has seen
his eyelids full of it

The women
aching to heal their men
unable

The hundreds in their safe and tidy houses
along the shore
What of them?

They watched and listened
saw and heard too much
images
    from things seen
    things imagined
    things reported
the sea sinister
the wind a sigh ·a shriek
a voice that weeps and goes on weeping
(there's a lot of wind around St. Margaret's Bay)
people without voices
crying out for connection
for something to give a face
to their strange unidentified grief

And in the meantime
in distant places
the families
the loved ones
were pushing against the thoughts
that were dragging them under
drowning in loss
and discovering
that the wound they thought had been healing
was gaping
wide open again

And so it can be
with a pain that lies deep in the spirit
eroding the barrier door
no matter how strong the metal
and from time to time
escaping into their minds
in a troubled present
heavy with anguish

So thus was formed
a unique community of need
moving from far-flung lands
where live the loved ones
into the Lord Nelson Hotel
and the city of Halifax
reaching beyond the bounds
of villages  of towns
out onto the toiling ships
with the men who searched the sea
week after week

onto the *Preserver* the *Grapple* the ghostly barge
and with the Coast Guard Auxiliary
into the tents and trailers
that housed the searchers
to the kitchens of women
who hoped that a Black Forest cake
a box of chocolate squares (topped with nuts)
could form a link with at least
one other

Finally gradually
real bridges were built
joining helper to griever
talking to silence
touching with hands with words
with mute understanding

From Switzerland from the States
from more exotic places
came and returned the pilgrims
year upon year
in summer in chilly fall
in cheerless winter
reaching back and again back
to feel once more that link
of common experience
that large community of caring

And with this link this odd affiliation
there came for us the knowing
the mild surprise of knowing
that we needed those families

those grieving loved ones
as much
as they still needed us

And so it was
(at least for some)
in slow unstructured ways
surprising us with warmth
with rare and deep affection
we met each other

And swept by shifting currents
of the spirit
their course uncharted by intention
unplotted  unexpected
in ways defying logic or belief
the sea change came full circle

## September 2015

Listen
far off in the distance
the voice of a foghorn
always a sound full of questions
containing a sorrow and fear
but oddly a comfort
   with a rise and fall
   like the waves
sorrow and fear and a comfort
speaking together

But today  with a sudden breeze
out of the west
the sun is already the winner
striking the new yellow paint
   on Lawson's two fish stores
   the bright machinery on the Government Wharf
   and the morning wash
      as it sails out the line
the boats are humming and coughing
their motors are grumbling
poised for another day
   of checking equipment
   harvesting mackerel
   feeding the tuna

and out on the Government Wharf
the kids are fishing
fishing with hand-fashioned gear
hauling in pollock

eager to squeeze from each day
the gifts that are theirs
before facing the fact of the autumn
   the spectre of school
   and the end of their freedom

While back in the kitchens
the women are rushing
   to clear up the dishes
   or package the lunches
before they jump in the cars
   for their jobs or their errands
   or into the boats
    with their men
   kids arrive to the sitters
   or sitters for kids
    or maybe the elderly parents
   nothing is still
   everything urgent
   all is in motion

But before very long
out on the water
the vessels are fast disappearing
are melting
into the path
of their wide band of sunshine
onto the eastern horizon
even the sound of their engines
is suddenly mute
swallowed by distance and light

I watch from the wharf
and I know
there's an end and another beginning

The end of a night that was long

But day has begun

# Acknowledgements

There may be those who wonder why, for so small a book, it has been necessary to thank so many people. But more than seventeen years have passed since the Swissair crash, and that is a long time. As a result, I have spoken with many men and women who were involved in the aftermath of the tragedy. I have heard their personal stories, their descriptions of weather, equipment, circumstances, and individual trauma. I have seen a lot of things with my own eyes, but I have also been informed, advised, given suggestions, comforted, and inspired by a great many people – families of the victims, workers on land and sea, observers, professional people with enormous responsibilities, local inhabitants, military personnel, and some who have been severely damaged by their own experiences.

Most of the people mentioned in the account have read the manuscript, as I felt I should get their permission to use their names. For some, this was easy to do, and sometimes they offered useful suggestions or factual corrections. For others, reading the text was a difficult task, as they struggled with the troubling memories that were reignited by some of the poems. Most allowed their names to be used – but not all. For a variety of reasons, they preferred to remain anonymous.

I thank all of the people I interviewed, more than I can possibly express. As well as assisting me in achieving my own recovery from an experience that had certainly wounded me, they helped me to reach some sort of balance in my view of the total picture. Some of those people showed great patience and kindness when I kept returning to them again and again with more questions. John O'Donnell, for instance, must have become very tired of answering my phone calls and e-mails, but he never once showed any impatience – just as he had demonstrated the same generosity of spirit throughout his weeks of service, religious and secular, to the whole community. Judge Lorne Clarke was equally accessible and ready to offer help to anyone in need of relevant information or counsel.

Dr. John Butt, Chief Medical Officer of the Province of Nova Scotia at that time, with a mountain of responsibilities that would have daunted most people in his professional position, kept important focus on his prime task, while finding – somehow – the time and energy to comfort the families personally, and to console so many people individually. I will always be especially grateful to him for his supportive and generous conversation with me, sixteen long years after the crash, bringing the wheel full circle for me in a way he may not even have realized at the time.

I also feel enormous gratitude to Commander Rick Town – now Captain (RCN) Rick Town (Retired) – for his open and honest letters. They comforted and also significantly strengthened me; and I give very sincere thanks to this thoughtful and generous man – still on the pinnacle of that pyramid mentioned in my text.

Many thanks to members of the Swissair families who, as well as having contributed to this book, have become important people in my life: Claire Mortimer, the Wilkins family, Nancy Wight, Nancy Hausman, to name only a few. They opened up my mysterious grief, and gave meaning to my sadness. They are valued friends.

I thank Peggy and Robert Conrad for our many talks, and for their friendship. I appreciate their hospitality and warmth, and their readiness to answer a lot of questions that have helped me in the writing of these poems. I also thank Marshall Boutilier, another local fisherman, whose description of the weather and sea on that first night made the background scene vivid to me in a way that no one else was able to do. His wife, Sheila, also made that terrible Wednesday come alive for me in a new way.

There are so many people to thank: my friend Cynthia Martin, with her countless muffins; Lesa Griffin, now Director of Sales at the Lord Nelson Hotel, who proved to me that the simplest gesture of kindness can have a profound effect; Dawn Upshaw, who put in motion a musical mission that will live forever in the hearts of those who witnessed it; Sister Dorothy Moore, whose words produced a change in my spirit – for which no thanks will ever be enough; Bart Strak (of the poem "The Morgue") – now head of all the Aeromedical Operations in the Northwest Territories and the Kitikmeot Region of Nunavut – who was so open and generous in his description of his individual suffering, and so willing to let me use my account exactly as I wrote it; Barb Robson, who organized the army of women who made Nancy Wight's quilt, and whose own originally designed and very beautiful quilt (entitled Sea Change) is – by my choice – on the cover of this book; Debra Paquin, and her extraordinary gift of heart-shaped stones, which lifted that dark cloud from above our heads, not once, but twice, when it was so sorely needed; and Lorri Neilsen Glenn, who – as a friend and teacher – has enriched my life in many ways, and who gave us the "moving Christmas lights" as the Emergency vehicles travelled down Highway 329 on the night of September 2, 1998.

The list doesn't stop there. I also conferred with many people who do not appear in the manuscript. I thank Marlene Hudson and David Turnbull of the staff of the Lord Nelson Hotel, who cheerfully took time away from their work to give me important information on the ways in which that hotel provided care and comfort to the Swissair families. I consulted my friend Sister Kate Waters, who discussed various ethical matters with me in connection with this book. Don Connolly, host of CBC's *Information Morning*, answered my questions and spoke to me several times about the disaster – and also about the media's role in broadcasting information about it. He did this with care and sensitivity, as did two other CBC staff members who did not wish to be named.

Jane Kansas of the CBC (but not on duty that evening) had accompanied the CBC reporters to Peggy's Cove, and later described for me the scene on the sea as she witnessed it from the base of the lighthouse for most of that night. A similar description – but from the other side of the Bay – was given me by Sandy Lutwick who lived on Owl's Head at that time. Both accounts helped to bring the words "a fearsome beauty" and "Armageddon" to my mind.

Sylvia Gunnery – right from the beginning, from September 1998 onwards – listened to me with kindness and patience whenever I wanted or needed to talk about the crash. Kirsten Franklin, whose interest in Swissair and in my project has been constant, combed the Internet for specific factual information I needed, believed in my text from the first time she read it, and encouraged me many times when I was low in spirit and confidence. Her many conversations with me about the tragedy have been – and continue to be – both sensitive and therapeutic.

I wanted to start the Acknowledgements with a tribute to Eileen Richmond, but she refused to be first in line. I will therefore do it now. Eileen has been much more than just "my typist." She took my handwritten work – with its odd spacing, its lack of punctuation, and its inconsistent indentations – interpreted everything with accuracy and sensitivity, and then committed all of it to her computer. She was also almost the first person to whom I spoke about the subject matter of the text and my goals. She gets five stars for her listening skills and for her understanding of what I was trying to do. Only once did she enter the area of composition, but when she did, I acted on her suggestion, thereby creating a significant improvement to the work as a whole. In all she has done for me, she has been perceptive and wise as well as skillful.

I'd like to make particular mention of Stephen Kimber and his wonderful book *Flight 111: The Tragedy of the Swissair Crash*, released within one year of the crash, but containing an astonishing wealth of dependable information about events before and after the disaster – key people, the airline itself and its intricate reactions, and early manoeuvres of the Transport Safety Board. Special thanks to him for providing such a valuable resource.

I would like to thank the team at Pottersfield Press for their sensitive efficiency in the publishing of *After Swissair*: Lesley Choyce for his swift acceptance of the manuscript, and his cooperation in all matters leading up to its becoming a book; Julia Swan, the book's editor, for her careful and thoughtful attention to detail and for listening to my point of view at all times; Gail LeBlanc for supporting my choice of a cover, and making it a reality; and Peggy Amirault, without whose layout work the book would not exist as it is today.

My own family deserves all the praise and thanks I can give them. It is not often easy to live with someone who is writing a book of any kind.

He or she disappears into the work and tends to neglect everything and everyone else – except when specifically needed. But writing this book – even just *thinking* about it during the many months when circumstances prevented actual work on it – caused me a lot of residual pain and stress which must have spun off my material into the air around me. I know that the tension also moved onto the e-mail and phone lines of those family members who were absent. I'm extremely grateful to them for putting up with all of that for so long – and without complaint. My love and thanks to all three of them – Alan, Glynis, and Andrea.

# Appendix

## One Year After the Crash

### CBC Commentary Script
### September 2, 1999
### Budge Wilson

We are a different people because of what we have seen, or heard, or imagined. Nova Scotians, and particularly those living along the shores nearby, know that they have suffered a sea change.

Who could have believed that we would feel so much and so deeply for people we had never met? How could we have foreseen that the experience would alter our reaction to the movement of the sea or the sound of the wind? And who could have imagined that it would take us so many months to emerge from under that heavy cloud?

But now I am full of wonder at the positive experience that arose out of that dreadful event and at my new awareness of the potential for courage and generosity among us. We have found ourselves to be part of an enormous family, made up of the fishermen who combed the sea for survivors on that first awful night; the brave divers who walked amongst wreckage as sharp and as lethal as razor · blades; the countless men and women who searched, and found, and retrieved; Dr. Butt's valiant crew at the Shearwater morgue; the army of women who baked and comforted; the sensitive members of the media who saw and knew much more than they told; the counsellors who listened to terrible tales; and the hundreds of others who helped and suffered.

This was a family to be proud of. The *real* family members of the victims of that crash need never worry lest their loved ones be forgotten. Those people are part of our memory and of our emotional history, and will remain so.

For most of us, the sea is beautiful once more, the wind no longer the moan of remembered anguish. But we Nova Scotians have had to factor Swissair One Eleven into our daily lives, and we know that it will continue to be part of our future. Like the Ancient Mariner, we have told our story over and over again, hoping for relief from the pain that has inhabited us for so long.

So the tragedy lingers on. But in the process of our grieving, we have learned that sometimes the human spirit can be unselfish and heroic to a degree that has astonished us.

This does not spell the end of our mourning. But a shaft of light has begun to focus upon the dark and troubled sea of our sadness. On this particular day, we need to pay attention to that light and to draw strength from it.

# The Sea Change Quilt

## Barb Robson

On the first anniversary of the Swissair Fight 111 plane crash, I heard Budge Wilson's commentary on CBC. She talked about the "sea change" that had taken place in our community along the Aspotogan Peninsula. I knew I wanted to try and put her words into a quilt – Sea Change is the result.

It is the first in a series of three quilts that for me commemorate those early years after the crash. We had not lived long in the community but we quickly became part of it. We met some incredible people and became lifelong friends with two of the Swissair families.

My quilt Sea Change is meant to subtly illustrate the effect on the families in our community as well as the families of those who lost their lives. I used the traditional "log cabin" quilt block (which represents the home), but pieced it in a rather chaotic way to reflect the upheaval in so many lives. The circles represent the ocean, always changing and yet in a way comforting.

Sea Change is an original design, machine pieced, hand appliquéd and hand quilted. It is 24½ inches by 24½ inches and the fabrics are 100 percent cotton.

Barb Robson's website is www.barbrobson.com.

# About the Author

Budge Wilson was born and educated in Nova Scotia, but spent many years in Ontario, returning home in 1989. She lives in a South Shore fishing village. She has had a varied career – best known as a writer for children and young adults, she has been a teacher, commerical artist, illustrator, photographer, and fitness instructor.

A very late bloomer, she began writing fiction in her fifties and published her first book in 1984 when she was 56. She has now published 33 books, with 27 foreign editions in 14 languages – and has appeared in over 90 anthologies. Her books for children and teens range from picture books to novels for middle schoolers to young adult novels. Her most recent book is *Before Green Gables*, a prequel to the iconic Anne of Green Gables books, published by Penguin in 2008. It has been published in 11 countries and 7 languages, with a Japanese animation, and was recognized by *Quill & Quire* as one of the "Best Books of 2008." Her books for adults are short story collections. *After Swissair* is her first collection of poetry.

Wilson's work has received much crtiical acclaim. She has received 21 Canadian Children's Book Centre "Our Choice" Awards. *The Leaving* was featured on the American Library Association's 1994 list of "The 75 best children's books of the last 25 years." Her books have won several literary prizes including the Ann Connor Brimer Award and the Canadian Library Association Young Adult Award. And she has been nominated for the Raddall Atlantic Fiction Prize, the Commonwealth Prize, the Governor General's Award, the CBA's Libris Children's Author of the Year Award, CLA's Best Children's Book Award, and for the Ruth and Sylvia Schwartz Award.

She has also received honorary degrees from Dalhousie and Mount Saint Vincent universities. In 2003, she received the Halifax Mayor's Award for Cultural Achievement. In 2004, Wilson was made a Member of the Order of Canada, and in 2011, she was inducted into the Order of Nova Scotia for her contributions to Canadian and Nova Scotia writing.

## Books by Budge Wilson

### Fiction for Adults and Young Adults

*Before Green Gables*
*Friendships: Stories*
*Fractures: Family Stories*
*Mothers & Other Strangers*
*The Dandelion Garden*
*Cordelia Clark*
*The Courtship and Other Stories*
*The Leaving*

### Books for Young People of All Ages

*Izzie: Book One, The Christmas That Almost Wasn't*
*Izzie: Book Two, Trongate Fury*
*Izzie: Book Three, Patricia's Secret*
*Izzie: Book Four, Homecoming*
*The Imperfect Perfect Christmas. Illustrated by Terry Roscoe*
*A Fiddle for Angus. Illustrated by Susan Tooke*
*Manfred, The Unmanageable Monster. Illustrated by Jill Quinn*

*Duff's Monkey Business. Illustrated by Kim LaFave*

*The Fear of Angelina Domino. Illustrated by Eugenie
    Fernandes*

*The Cat That Barked. Illustrated by Terry Roscoe*

*Sharla*

*The Long Wait. Illustrated by Eugenie Fernandes*

*Duff the Giant Killer. Illustrated by Kim LaFave*

*Harold and Harold. Illustrated by Terry Roscoe*

*Cassandra's Driftwood. Illustrated by Terry Roscoe*

*Oliver's Wars*

*Lorinda's Diary*

*Madame Belzile and Ramsay Hitherton-Hobbs.
    Illustrated by Etta Moffatt*

*Going Bananas. Illustrated by Graham Pilsworth*

*Thirteen Never Changes*

*Breakdown*

*Mystery Lights at Blue Harbour*

*A House Far from Home*

*The Best/Worst Christmas Present Ever*

*Mr. John Bertrand Nijinsky and Charlie. Illustrated by
    Terry Roscoe*